A DORLING KINDERSLEY BOOK

Editor Lara Tankel Holtz
Designer Helen Melville
Managing Editor Sheila Hanly
Production Catherine Semark
Illustrator Ellis Nadler
Photography Mike Dunning
Additional photography
Finbar Hawkins, Ray Moller
Consultant John Poulter

First published in Great Britain in 1995
by Dorling Kindersley Limited,
9 Henrietta Street, London WC2E 8PS

A CIP catalogue record for this book is available
from the British Library.

ISBN: 0-7513-5136-9

Colour reproduction by Chromagraphics, Singapore
Printed in Italy by L.E.G.O.

Dorling Kindersley would like to thank
Goughs of Hunsingore, Greenland UK Ltd,
and Duncan Chapman for their help in
producing this book.

The publisher would like to thank the
following for their kind permission to
reproduce photographs:

Greenland UK Ltd: 14, 20
top centre World Pictures,
Feature Pix Colour
Library Ltd: 15 bottom right

Scale
Look out for drawings like
this – they show the size
of machines compared
with people.

Combine harvester
Page 12

Forage harvester
Page 15

Baler
Page 17

Farm loader
Page 18

Trailer
Page 20

Plough
Page 9

Mighty Machines

TRACTOR

Claire Llewellyn

Muck spreader
Page 11

Tractor
Page 6

DK

DORLING KINDERSLEY
LONDON • NEW YORK • STUTTGART

Tractor

The tractor is the most important machine on a farm. Its powerful engine helps it to pull along other machinery to do different jobs. Its large wheels stop it from getting stuck in the mud.

cab

7110 CASE INT

small front wheels swivel to turn the tractor

big tyres help the tractor to roll smoothly over bumps

ridges on the tyres grip ...pery mud

A **tyre** is a rubber ring fitted round a wheel and filled with air.

Hitched up

At the back of the tractor are three hitches. Other farm machines can be hooked on to these.

hitches are controlled by levers in the cab

headlight is turned on when the farmer drives at night

 Some tractors have a carpet, stereo, and even a cold drinks cabinet to keep the driver happy.

 The powerful engine gives the tractor the same pulling power of at least 200 horses.

 The tractor weighs up to 6 tonnes – that's as heavy as 230 seven-year-old children.

Scale

Preparing the soil

The farmer uses a tractor and plough to cut and turn the soil before planting a crop. The plough's steel blades dig deep into the soil and turn it over, leaving long grooves called furrows.

Scale

🔩 Race horses can run a 6.5 km race in 3 minutes. It would take a tractor and plough 25 minutes to go the same distance.

🔩 Some ploughs weigh 2 tonnes – as much as two family cars.

cab is high up so the driver can see all around

8 🔩 A **blade** is a sharp edge usually used for cutting. 🔩 **Steel** is a hard, tough metal.

steel blades of
the power harrow
cut through
lumps of soil

Smoothing the bumps

The ground is very rough
after ploughing. The furrow
press smooths the bumpy soil
and the power harrow breaks
up the lumps.

furrow press

Horsepower (hp)

Before the tractor was
invented, ploughs were
pulled by horses. This
tractor has the pulling
power of 170 horses.
It is said to have a
170 hp engine.

blades turn
over soil

plough is hooked
to the back of
the tractor

Horsepower (hp) is the unit used to measure the strength of an engine.

Planting the crop

AMAZING FACTS ☼

A seed drill can sow a 30 acre field in one day. It would take one person at least a week to do the same thing.

Scale

mud guards stop flying mud getting into the machine

When the field is ready for planting, the farmer pours seeds into the seed drill. The drill's hollow blades scratch holes in the ground. Seeds drop through the blades into the holes and rods cover them in earth.

grooves in the tyre are about 5 cm deep

Seeds grow on plants. After they are sown in the ground they grow into new plants.

Muck spreader

The muck spreader spreads manure on to the field. Manure feeds the soil, helping plants to grow healthily.

seeds are blown down the tubes by a stream of air

hopper contains seeds, which drop through a hole at the bottom

Mucking about

Inside the muck spreader are fast-moving chains. They fling out lots of manure as the muck spreader moves along.

A **drill** is a tool for making holes. **Manure** is the waste matter of animals. 11

Combine harvester

The combine harvester does several jobs at once. It harvests, or cuts and gathers, the crop. It separates the grain from the straw and places the grain safely in the grain tank. The straw is spread in rows back on to the field to be collected later.

flashing light tells other vehicles to look out

Scale

Combined effort

In the huge wheat fields of Canada and the United States, teams of combines work together to harvest a single field.

big window gives the farmer a clear view of the cutter bar

MASSEY FERGUSON

razor-sharp blades

  The **grain** is the small, hard seed of a cereal plant such as wheat.

Threshing the crop

In the threshing cylinder the freshly cut crop is threshed, or shaken, until the grain drops off the stalk.

grain tank

threshing cylinder

MASSEY FERGUSON

funnel can move up and down

a tank of grain pours out of the funnel in less than two minutes

AMAZING FACTS

The grain tank holds 6,000 kilograms of grain – that's enough to make 7,400 loaves of bread.

The combine can cut a strip more than 6.5 metres wide – it would take 16 garden lawn mowers to cut the same width.

Harvesting the forage

Crops that farmers feed to their animals in winter, such as grass, are called forage. The grass for forage is cut by a mower. Inside the mower the grass is squashed between rollers to squeeze out the water. It is then left to dry in the sun.

Scale

swath

After grass has been mowed it is left in neat bands called **swaths**.

shredded grass
is blown out
of the funnel

Forage harvester

When the mown grass
is dry and wilted, the
farmer picks it up with a
forage harvester. This has
a pick-up bar to lift the grass
into the blades to chop it.

pick-up
bar

AMAZING FACTS

⬤ The pick-up bar has
24 blades. Each rotates
1,000 times a minute,
cutting and chopping
everything in its path.

⬤ The mower is 3.2
metres wide – as wide
as you and two friends
lying head to toe.

⬤ A forage harvester's
engine is as powerful
as 400 horses.

Harvesting rice

Rice is grown in a flooded field called a paddy field.
The rice harvester chops down the rice plants and
collects the grains in a storage box. This harvester
is small so that it does not sink in the soft fields.

A **funnel** is a tube that is used to move things from one container to another. 15

Hay making

Hay is fed to animals in the winter. It is made from grass that farmers have left to dry in the fields. A hay bob is used to flick and turn over the hay. When the hay is bone dry it can be gathered and made into bales.

Scale

⬡ A hay bale weighs up to 300 kg – it would take five tough football players to lift it.

⬡ A baler can tie up a bale with twine in 10 seconds.

gases from the engine are cleaned by this filter

exhaust pipe

699   MASSEY FERGUSON

steps up to tractor cab

🔩 Gases from the engine are forced out through the **exhaust pipe.** ⬡⬡⬡

bale chamber where the bale is tied up

Baler
The baler rolls along the ground and collects loose hay. Once it's inside the machine, spinning rollers wind the hay into a tight bale.

bale wrapper

The wrapper
A bale wrapper wraps damp grass in plastic – it is then used for animal food called silage.

spinning rollers

KRONE

back tyres carry the weight of the bales

long handle to help farmer move hay rake

long metal fingers gather the grass into rows ready for baling

KS 3.50 / 10

A **hay bale** is a tightly-packed bundle of hay tied up with twine or string.

17

Lifting and carrying

Special vehicles are used by the farmer to lift and carry loads all over the farm. A farm loader speeds along quickly, shifting heavy loads of grain or manure from place to place. The loader is very small, so it can be driven through barn doors and along narrow paths.

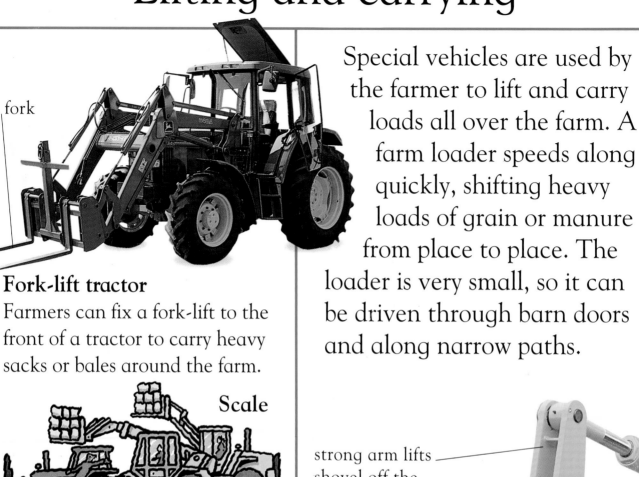

fork

Fork-lift tractor
Farmers can fix a fork-lift to the front of a tractor to carry heavy sacks or bales around the farm.

Scale

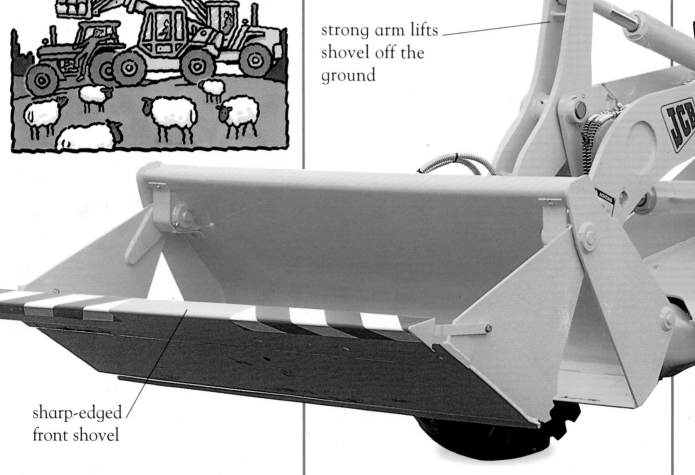

strong arm lifts shovel off the ground

JCB

sharp-edged front shovel

Forks are long prongs that slide under a load and lift it off the ground.

Long arm

A telescopic handler lifts and stacks hay bales. Its arm slides out like a telescope, getting longer and longer until it reaches the very top of the hay stack.

arm

forks are used to lift hay bales

glass doors so driver can see all around

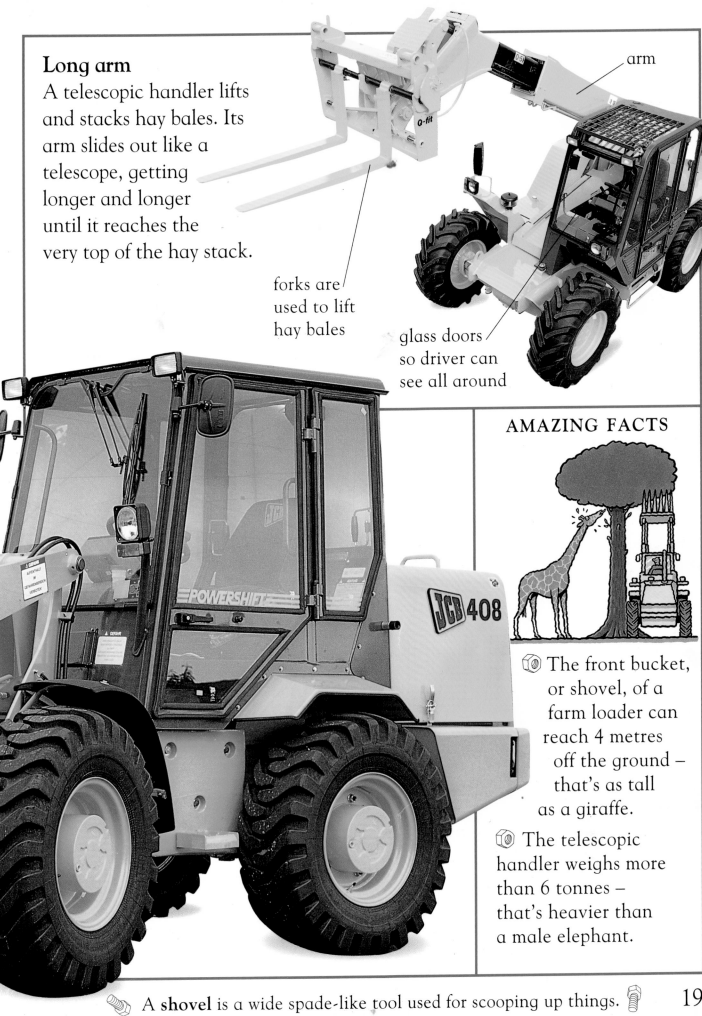

POWERSHIFT

JCB 408

AMAZING FACTS

The front bucket, or shovel, of a farm loader can reach 4 metres off the ground – that's as tall as a giraffe.

The telescopic handler weighs more than 6 tonnes – that's heavier than a male elephant.

A **shovel** is a wide spade-like tool used for scooping up things.

Loading up

AMAZING FACTS

The longest trailers are over 8 metres long – big enough to hold a 15 person brass band and all their instruments!

The trailer carries 16 tonnes – more than three big elephants.

For big, awkward loads the farmer uses a variety of vehicles. A trailer hitched to the back of a tractor is used to move loose grain from the field to the storage area. Pistons raise up one end of the trailer so it can empty its heavy load.

Scale

piston

hatch slides up to let the grain pour out

20 A **piston** is a metal tube that fits inside a bigger tube and slides in and out.

Horsebox

For a long journey, a horse needs to ride in a horsebox. The back of the box is on hinges, and drops down to make a gentle slope for the horse to walk up.

front is attached to a car or truck

trailer is raised high off the ground and the load is tipped out

mirror allows driver to see behind trailer

tractor pulls along trailer

All-terrain vehicle

These sturdy vehicles can travel over any sort of ground. In Australia, the all-terrain vehicle is often used for rounding up sheep.

Multipurpose

The multipurpose truck is built to carry heavy loads and can even pull a plough.

Terrain is any type of ground – from rocky mountains to sandy deserts.

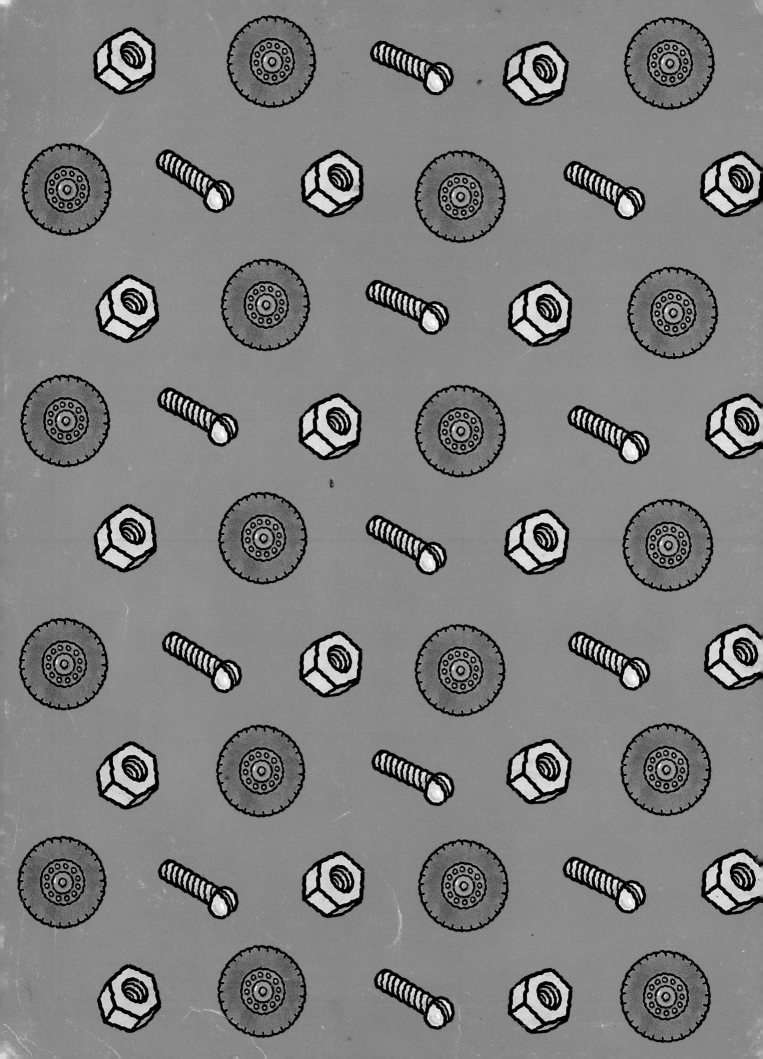